UNCOVERING AMERICAN HISTORY™

A PRIMARY SOURCE INVESTIGATION OF THE ALAMO

SUSANNA KELLER
AND JANEY LEVY

rosen publishing's
rosen central®

Published in 2016 by The Rosen Publishing Group, Inc.
29 East 21st Street, New York, NY 10010

First Edition

Library of Congress Cataloging-in-Publication Data

Keller, Susanna.
A primary source investigation of the Alamo/Susanna Keller and Janey Levy.—First edition.
pages cm.—(Uncovering American history)
Includes bibliographical references and index.
ISBN 978-1-4994-3507-8 (library bound)
1. Alamo (San Antonio, Tex.)—History—Sources—Juvenile literature.
2. Alamo (San Antonio, Tex.)—Siege, 1836—Sources—Juvenile literature.
3. San Antonio (Tex.)—History—Sources—Juvenile literature. I. Levy, Janey.
II. Title.
F394.S2118K45 2016
976.4'03—dc23

2014043160

Manufactured in the United States of America

CONTENTS

INTRODUCTION

"Remember the Alamo!" is one of the most famous rallying cries in American history. The phrase dates back to the Battle of the Alamo, which was fought in 1836 in San Antonio, Texas. The battle and the siege that led up to it were key events in the Texas Revolution, also known as the Texas War of Independence. It was in this war that the settlers of Texas, most of whom came from the United States, fought for their independence from Mexico. The war led to the establishment of the Republic of Texas, which remained an independent state until 1845, when it joined the United States as the country's twenty-eighth state.

The battle was fought between Mexican troops and a small group of settlers who had taken up a defensive position in the Alamo, a compound of buildings that had started out as a Spanish mission. The settlers were badly outnumbered, but they held their ground in the belief that doing so would help Texas win its independence. The defenders paid a high cost for their loyalty to their cause; all of them were killed when the Mexican forces stormed the Alamo early on the morning of March 6,

1836. However, their sacrifice made the defenders heroes to the people of Texas, inspiring a deep dedication to the cause of Texas independence. In fact, cries to "Remember the Alamo!" were heard that April, in the deciding battle of the war.

The defenders' self-sacrifice and willingness to fight against insurmountable odds continues to inspire people, both in Texas and across the United States. Today the Alamo is a popular tourist destination, one that holds a unique place in the American imagination.

★ CHAPTER ONE

THE ALAMO'S BEGINNINGS

The first people to live in what is now the San Antonio area were Native American. In the 1500s, the area was home to the Coahuiltecans, a mix of groups who lived in southern Texas and northeastern Mexico. They were hunter-gatherers who lived in small family bands. The bands moved around with the seasons to find food, such as deer, rabbits, pecans, and mesquite bean pods. Sometimes, several bands would come together to trade or to make use of the same particularly abundant food resource. One Coahuiltecan group known to have lived in the San Antonio area was the Payayas.

THE SPANISH ARRIVE

The first European to reach the area was the Spanish captain Alonso Álvarez de Pineda, who sailed along the coast of what is now called the Gulf of Mexico in 1519. Nine years later, a shipwrecked Spaniard named Álvar Núñez Cabeza de Vaca explored the interior regions. He kept a journal of his experiences and published it in Spain in 1542 under the name *La relación* (*The Account*). In his journal, he described the land, the plant and animal life, and Native American groups he had encountered. Though Cabeza de Vaca's detailed account is now considered one of the most important sources for information about the native peoples of Texas, it failed to provoke much curiosity about the area at the time it was published. For the next century and a half, European explorers concerned themselves with other parts of the New World and paid little attention to the region.

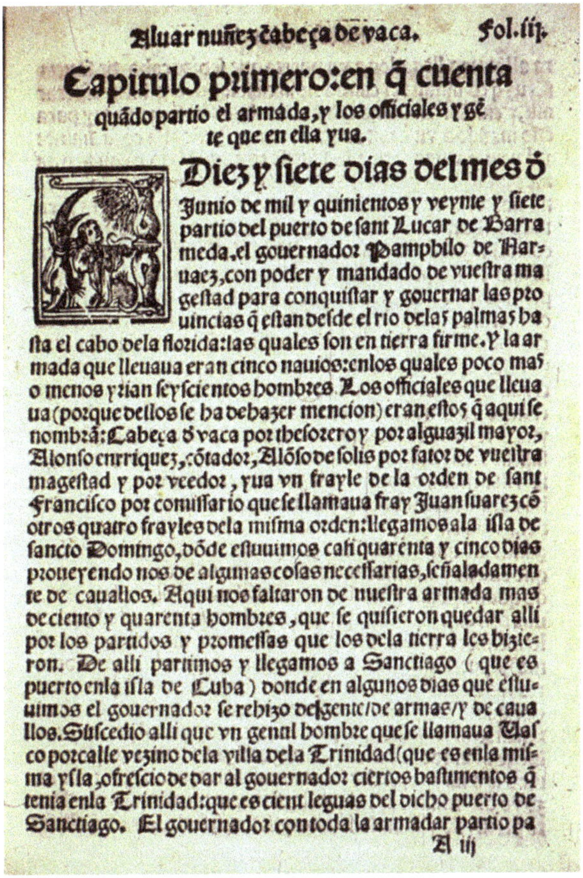

Aluar nuñez cabeça de vaca. Fol. iij.

Capitulo primero: en q̃ cuenta
quãdo partio el armada, y los officiales y gẽ
te que en ella yua.

Diez y siete dias del mes d
Junio de mil y quinientos y veynte y siete
partio del puerto de sant Lucar de Barra
meda, el gouernador Pamphilo de Nar-
uaez, con poder y mandado de vuestra ma
gestad para conquistar y gouernar las pro
uincias q̃ estan desde el rio de las palmas ha
sta el cabo dela florida: las quales son en tierra firme. Y la ar
mada que lleuaua eran cinco nauios: enlos quales poco mas
o menos yrian seyscientos hombres. Los officiales que lleua
ua (porque dellos se ha de hazer mencion) eran estos q̃ aqui se
nombrã: Cabeça d vaca por thesorero y por alguazil mayor,
Alonso enrriquez, cõtador, Alõso de solis por fator de vuestra
magestad y por veedor, yua vn frayle de la orden de sant
Francisco por comissario que se llamaua fray Juan suarez cõ
otros quatro frayles dela misma orden: llegamos ala isla de
sancto Domingo, dõde estuuimos casi quarenta y cinco dias
proueyendo nos de algunas cosas necessarias, señaladamen
te de cauallos. Aqui nos faltaron de nuestra armada mas
de ciento y quarenta hombres, que se quisieron quedar alli
por los partidos y promessas que los dela tierra les hizie-
ron. De alli partimos y llegamos a Sanctiago (que es
puerto enla isla de Cuba) donde en algunos dias que estu-
uimos el gouernador se rehizo de gente, de armas, y de caua
llos. Sucedio alli que vn gentil hombre que se llamaua Vas
co porcalle vezino dela villa dela Trinidad (que es enla mis-
ma ysla, ofrescio de dar al gouernador ciertos bastimentos q̃
tenia enla Trinidad: que es cient leguas del dicho puerto de
Sanctiago. El gouernador con toda la armada partio pa

A iij

This page from the first chapter of the 1555 edition of *La relación* tells how the expedition set off from Sanlúcar de Barrameda on June 17, 1527.

In 1685, the Spanish became more interested in the region after the French explorer René-Robert La Salle established a colony on the Gulf Coast. The French colony lasted only five years, but its presence caused the Spanish to take action to protect their claim to the territory. Spanish soldiers and Catholic missionaries established missions throughout what is now Texas and northeastern Mexico. The missions had three purposes: to convert the Native Americans to the Catholic faith, to spread Spanish civilization in the New World, and to keep other Europeans from settling in Spain's New World territories.

During this period, there were changes in the area's Native American population. Some Coahuiltecans settled in the Spanish missions, adopting a more Spanish way of life. By this point, many Coahuiltecan groups had already been weakened or shattered by diseases introduced by the Spanish. Another destabilizing factor was the arrival of various intruders, both Spanish and Native American, into the areas in which the Coahuiltecans lived. By the late seventeenth century, the Lipan Apaches, who were themselves being pushed out of the southern Great Plains by

George Catlin's *Comanche Feats of Martial Horsemanship* dates from 1834. Catlin visited the Great Plains and made hundreds of paintings of the Native Americans living there.

the Comanches, had moved into the region. The Apaches had traditionally moved around throughout the year, following buffalo herds. After the Spanish introduced the horse to North America, the Apache became great riders and pursued their quarry on horseback. Upon reaching South Texas many Apache bands had begun to spend part of the year in one place, raising corn, beans, pumpkins, and melons. The Apaches became the dominant people in the region, driving out or absorbing native peoples who had preceded them.

In the early 1700s, though, the Comanches began to move into South Texas. As was the case with the Apaches, horses had become central to Comanche culture. The Comanches used their horses to hunt buffalo and wage war against other tribes. They also raided Spanish settlements, stole horses, and kidnapped women and children. Though their enemies feared them, the Comanches were also respected for their skill as traders and for their horsemanship. Their society was democratic, and each person had great individual freedom.

MISSION SAN ANTONIO DE VALERO

In 1718, Spanish soldiers and missionaries set up a fort of San Fernando de Béxar and a mission of San Antonio de Valero along the San Antonio River, in what is now the city of San Antonio, Texas. The mission's church, the building known today as the Alamo, was begun in 1744 but was never completed.

In 1749, some Apaches made peace with the Spanish in a ceremony at Mission San Antonio. They agreed to become Christians in exchange for Spanish protection

SPANISH MISSIONS

Spanish missions were compounds on the frontiers of Mexico. They aimed to convince Native Americans to settle in permanent communities and adopt a Spanish lifestyle. This included converting to Catholicism, adopting Spanish farming practices (such as irrigation), and learning Spanish trades, such as carpentry, weaving, and blacksmithing. Most missions had herds of cattle, sheep, and goats to provide meat, milk, wool, and hides for leather. Some Native Americans chose to keep their traditional ways of life over the regimented life on the missions. However, others valued the protection missions offered and the regular food supply they produced, especially since most native groups had been ravaged by European diseases.

Mission San Antonio de Valero, which would become known as the Alamo, was the first of several missions in the San Antonio area. These included San José y San Miguel de Aguayo, Nuestra Señora de la Purísima Concepción, San Juan Capistrano, and San Francisco de la Espada. The Spanish established a presidio, or fortified military post, nearby to defend the missions against attacks form the Apaches and, later, the Comanches.

against the Comanches. Other Apaches, however, continued to raid the missions. The Comanches also continued their efforts to drive out the intruders.

The mission was secularized in 1793. This means control of the mission passed from the church to local authorities. A company of Spanish soldiers from Mexico moved into the mission in 1803. According to historians, this is probably when the name "Alamo" was first used for the mission. The soldiers may have named it after the Mexican village they had come from: El Alamo. Also, the mission was surrounded by cottonwood trees, and the Spanish word for cottonwood is *alamo*.

By 1811, some Spanish leaders in Mexico had become unhappy with the way Spain was ruling Mexico, and they began to seek independence. Finally, in 1821, a revolution led by Agustín de Iturbide, an officer in the Spanish army, led to Mexico's independence. Iturbide then made himself president of the new nation, which included Texas. The following year, Iturbide made himself emperor. Iturbide proved to be a bad leader: he put those who did not agree with him into prison, shut down the Mexican congress, spent large amounts of money on himself, and completely ignored the unhappiness of the Mexican people.

This anonymous painting of Agustín de Iturbide was painted after he became emperor in 1822.

After gaining independence from Spain, the Mexican government signed peace treaties with all the Apaches. However, even as the Mexicans and the Apaches were making peace, the Comanches continued to threaten Mexican settlers in Texas. The Mexican government found it difficult to defend against the Comanches.

In 1820, Texas had only 4,000 Mexican settlers, mostly concentrated around San Antonio de Béxar (the community around the Mission San Antonio de Valero and the fort of San Fernando de Béxar), Goliad (east of San Antonio), and Nacogdoches (northeast of San Antonio, near the Louisiana border). There were too few of them to defend the vast empty spaces of Texas, and the Spanish government was unable to persuade more Mexicans to settle there. Most Mexicans thought the land in central Mexico was more valuable than the land in Texas. Finally, the Spanish government decided to allow settlers from the United States to come to Texas, hoping that these Anglo (white, non-Spanish) settlers would create a buffer zone that would help protect the Mexicans from Comanche attacks.

★ CHAPTER TWO

ANGLO SETTLERS ARRIVE

In 1819, Missouri entrepreneur Moses Austin was looking for an opportunity that would help him recover from recent financial setbacks. He decided that sparsely populated Texas offered great opportunities to someone who was willing to work hard. In 1820, he traveled to San Antonio to seek the Spanish governor's permission to establish a colony. Austin persuaded Governor Antonio María Martínez to write to Commandant General Joaquín de Arredondo, recommending that Austin be permitted to carry out his plan. To secure approval, Austin gave his assurance that the settlers would all be Catholic, even though this was not true. Austin also promised that the settlers would bring documents certifying their good conduct. While he waited for an answer, Austin returned to his home in Missouri. The wet, cold weather during the four-week journey left Austin with pneumonia.

TENSION IN TEXAS

In January 1821, Ambrosio María de Aldasoro, a member of Arredondo's council, wrote a letter to

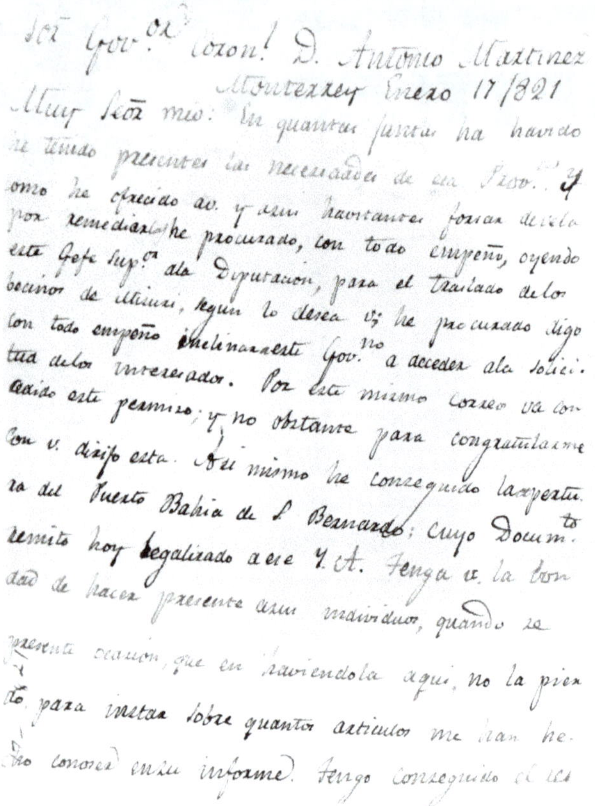
Sor. Gov.or Coron.l D. Antonio Martinez
Monterrey Enero 17/1821
Muy Señor mio: En quantas juntas ha havido he tenido presentes las necesidades de esa Prov.a y como he ofrecido a v. y a sus havitantes forzar de ela por remediarlas, he procurado, con todo empeño, oyendo este Gefe Sup.or ala Diputacion, para el traslado de los vecinos de [illegible], segun lo desea v.; he procurado digo con todo empeño [illegible] Gov.no a acceder ala solicitud de los interesados. Por este mismo correo va concedido este permiso; y no obstante para congratularme con v. dirijo esta. Asi mismo he conseguido la apertura del Puerto Bahia de S. Bernardo; cuyo Docum.to remito hoy legalizado a ese Y. Ct. Tenga v. la bondad de hacer presente a sus individuos, quando se presente ocasion, que en haviendola aqui, no la pierdo para instar sobre quantos articulos me han hecho conocer en su informe. Tengo conseguido el [illegible]

Aldasoro's letter to Governor Martínez delivered the official approval for Anglo settlement in Texas. (For a transcription, please see p. 51.)

Governor Martínez, granting Austin permission to establish his colony. When Austin received word, he immediately began preparations for the undertaking. However, the effort proved too much for him. Weakened by the pneumonia, he died in Missouri on June 10, 1821, before he could realize his dream. On his deathbed, Moses Austin asked his wife to tell their twenty-eight-year-old son, Stephen, that his last request was that Stephen establish the Texas colony. Stephen immediately set about completing the plans for the settlers' journey to Texas. In January 1822, Stephen and three hundred Missouri families settled on the fertile land between the Colorado and Brazos Rivers in southeastern Texas. Problems with the Mexican government arose immediately. When Moses Austin had received permission for the colony in 1821, it was from the Spanish government, which then controlled Mexico. The government of newly independent Mexico, headed by Agustín de Iturbide, did not recognize the Anglo settlers' right to establish a colony.

Stephen Austin traveled to Mexico City, where he persuaded the Mexican government to grant permission for his colony. Stephen also had himself named *empresario*, or administrative agent, for the colony. As *empresario*, he was responsible for controlling immigration into the colony, setting up the legal system, distributing land to settlers, and overseeing the building of roads, schools, sawmills, and granaries. He was also responsible for representing the settlers' interests and concerns to the Mexican government. To ensure that the colony's lands were divided according to Mexican law, the area had to be mapped and surveyed. Austin and two surveyors, Nicholas Rightor and Horatio Chriesman, made maps of the region around 1822.

William Howard painted this portrait of Stephen Austin in Mexico City in 1833. It is a watercolor painted on ivory.

In spite of Stephen Austin's skillful diplomacy, tensions grew between the Anglo settlers in Texas and the Mexican government. The settlers' own actions contributed to the problems. For example, even though Moses Austin had assured Governor Martínez that the settlers were Catholics, most were in fact Protestants and refused to become Catholics. The settlers also resisted speaking Spanish and obeying Mexican laws, including the law that abolished slavery. Most settlers insisted on keeping slaves.

Soon there were more Anglo settlers in Texas than Mexicans, and many people in Mexico grew alarmed. They feared that the U.S. Congress and Andrew Jackson, the U.S. president, would try to claim Texas as part of the United States. Because of this, in 1830, the Mexican congress made it illegal for more U.S. settlers to come into Texas. To move the government of Texas closer to Mexico City and

ANTONIO LÓPEZ DE SANTA ANNA

Antonio López de Santa Anna had fought alongside Agustín de Iturbide in the 1821 revolution. In 1828, he became the highest-ranking general in Mexico. His role in defeating Spain's attempt to reconquer Mexico in 1829 made him a national hero, and in 1833, he was overwhelmingly elected president of Mexico.

Unfortunately, Santa Anna was as bad a leader as Iturbide had been, and his actions contributed to the tensions between Mexico and the Anglo settlers. In 1834, he declared that Mexico was not ready for democracy and named himself dictator. The following year, Santa Anna increased his control by abolishing all local governments. He became angry when anyone resisted his authority, as the Anglo settlers did, and it was this anger that caused him to throw the visiting Stephen Austin into prison. The settlers deeply resented Santa Anna's actions, which they felt took away many of their rights.

Mexican control, Texas and the state of Coahuila, which bordered Texas to the south, were combined into a single state, with its capital deep inside Coahuila.

In 1832 and 1833, Anglo settlers gathered at San Felipe de Austin to protest the Mexican government's treatment of them and to propose that Texas be recognized as a Mexican state separate from Coahuila. In 1833, Stephen Austin traveled to Mexico City to discuss the settlers' concerns with the Mexican government. The trip ended with Austin being imprisoned for more than a year by the new president, Antonio López de Santa Anna.

THE BREAKING POINT

The situation worsened in October 1835. The residents of Gonzales, a small settlement east of San Antonio, had a small cannon, which the Mexican government had given them for defense against attacks by Native Americans. In punishment for the settlers' resistance to Santa Anna's government, the Mexican army demanded that the settlers surrender the cannon. Instead, the defiant settlers fired at the Mexicans. Enraged, Santa Anna sent General Martín Perfecto de Cos and several hundred soldiers to San Antonio to disarm all Texians and arrest anyone who opposed Santa Anna. The Texas war for independence had begun.

An army of settlers led by Stephen Austin laid siege to the Mexican troops in San Antonio de Béxar. The Anglo settlers finally launched a fierce attack on December 5, 1835. After five days of fighting, Cos surrendered and agreed to withdraw the Mexican troops and move south. About one hundred Anglo settlers then occupied the Alamo.

Sánchez Navarro created the only known image of the Alamo before the 1836 battle. This copy of that drawing is from the sketchbook of Jean-Louis Berlandier.

A diary left by José Juan Sánchez Navarro, an officer in the Mexican army, expresses their reaction to the defeat. On December 11, 1835, two days after the surrender of the Alamo, Sánchez Navarro wrote, " 'All has been lost save honor!' I do not remember, nor am I in the mood to remember, what French king said this, perhaps under better circumstances than those in which we are today, the eleventh of December, 1835. Béxar, and perhaps Texas has been lost." Sánchez Navarro was eager for revenge, and in February 1836 he wrote in his diary that Santa Anna had granted his request to return to the war in Texas.

While the Siege of Béxar was taking place, other Texians held a meeting known as the Consultation to discuss the situation. The Consultation became Texas's provisional government, meeting in Columbia in October and in San Felipe in November. The Nacogdoches representative was Samuel Houston. In December 1832, Houston had settled in

Nacogdoches, where he quickly became a leader of the community. By October 1835, Houston was convinced that war between the settlers and Mexico was inevitable. That same month, he was appointed commander in chief for the troops of the Nacogdoches region and issued a call for volunteers. On November 12, at the Consultation in San Felipe, Houston was appointed major general of the entire Texas army.

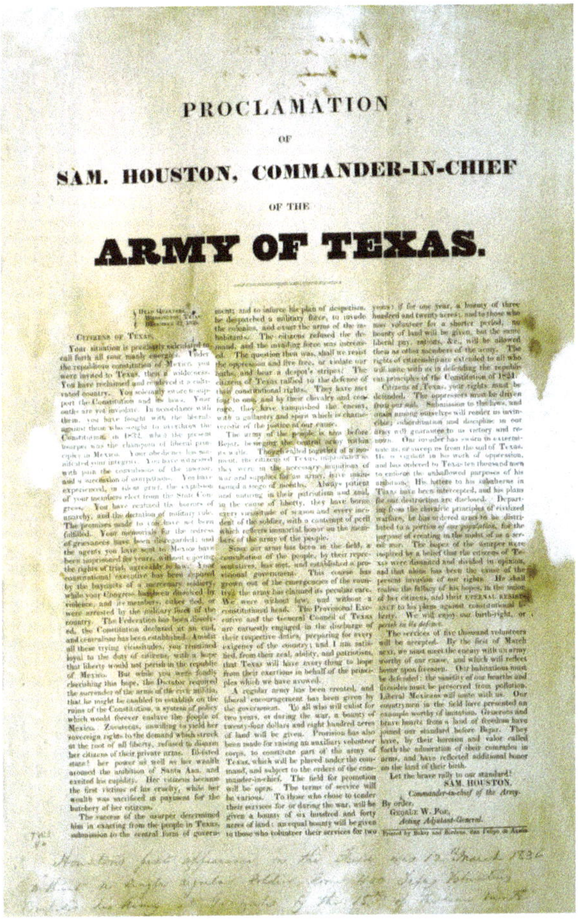

PROCLAMATION

OF

SAM. HOUSTON, COMMANDER-IN-CHIEF

OF THE

ARMY OF TEXAS.

Let the brave rally to our standard!

SAM. HOUSTON,

Commander-in-chief of the Army.

This broadside of Houston's request for reinforcements was printed by the firm of Baker and Bordens, in San Felipe de Austin. (For a transcription, please see pp. 51–52.)

One of Houston's first tasks as major general was to seek reinforcements for the Anglo troops occupying the Alamo. He knew that the Mexican army would attempt to retake the mission and that the small group of settlers would not be able to defend it. On December 12, 1835, only three days after the Anglo rebels had taken control of the Alamo, Houston issued a call for volunteers.

★ CHAPTER THREE

FAMOUS FIGURES

The men who responded to Houston's appeal for volunteers would go down in history as heroes of the Battle of the Alamo. Later lionizing accounts would turn them into larger-than-life heroes whose deeds exceeded anything that mortals could accomplish. While the truth is more complicated, there is no disputing that they were fascinating figures.

This portrait of David Crockett was painted by Chester Harding. Today it is in the National Portrait Gallery.

DAVID CROCKETT

Long before he arrived at the Alamo, David Crockett was a legend and folk hero. He had been born in Tennessee in 1786. He joined the Tennessee militia in 1813. Though poorly educated, Crockett

A LEGEND IN HIS OWN TIME

Though Crockett had some success as a politician, he really gained national fame as a sharpshooter, hunter, and storyteller. Even during his life, a number of works lionizing him were published. Playwright James Kirke Paulding based the hero of his play *The Lion of the West* on Crockett. The play was first performed in 1831. *Sketches and Eccentricities of Col. David Crockett of West Tennessee*, a book based on Crockett's adventures, was published in 1833. All this attention helped him win the congressional election later that year.

In 1834, *A Narrative of the Life of David Crockett of the State of Tennessee*, written by Crockett with the help of Thomas Chilton, was published. The following year, the first in a series of comic almanacs recounting outrageous tall tales about "Davy" Crockett appeared. The series continued until 1856.

became a justice of the peace in Lawrenceburg, Tennessee, in 1817. He was elected to the Tennessee legislature in 1821 and then to the U.S. House of Representatives in 1827. Crockett was defeated in his 1831 bid for reelection, but he won again in 1833.

The Whig Party considered nominating him as a presidential candidate to challenge President Andrew Jackson in the 1836 election, but it didn't happen in the end.

Disillusioned after he lost another bid for reelection to Congress in 1835, Crockett decided to explore Texas. If he found that it lived up to its reputation as a land full of opportunity, he would move his family there. On November 1, 1835, Crockett set out for Texas. Crockett was impressed with what he found. Texas "is the garden spot of the world," he wrote in a letter dated January 9, 1836. "I . . . have enrolled my name as a volunteer [to fight for Texas's independence] and will set out for the Rio Grand in a few days with the volunteers from the United States . . . I am in hopes of making a fortune yet for myself and family." Crockett reached San Antonio de Béxar in early February. There he met two other famous defenders of the Alamo, James Bowie and William Barret Travis.

JAMES BOWIE

Born in Kentucky in 1796, Bowie was a reckless, violent man whose pursuit of wealth and adventure led him to Texas. He served as a soldier in the War of 1812, which was fought between the United States and Britain for freedom of the seas. After the war, he was a slave trader, land speculator, and gambler. A large, physically powerful man, he was frequently involved in bloody fights. Tall tales were spread about him: he not only caught and rode wild horses, he also trapped bears and rode alligators.

Bowie arrived in Texas early in 1830. He married a wealthy woman and became involved in land speculation. His continuing search for wealth led him to conduct much business in Monclova, the new capital of Coahuila-Texas. When Santa Anna abolished local governments in May 1835 and ordered the arrest of foreigners doing business in Monclova, Bowie began to call for war with Mexico. He was too independent to join the regular army, but he led a small group of Texians who formed a militia, and he cooperated closely with Sam Houston.

Early in January 1836, Houston sent Bowie with thirty men to San Antonio de Béxar, with orders to destroy the Alamo. There were not enough men available to defend the Alamo, and Houston did not want the Mexican army to recapture the fort, which had become an important symbol of the Texas independence movement after the Texians drove out Cos and his soldiers. When Bowie reached the Alamo on January 19, he decided that it would be strategically important in the war for independence, and he did not follow Houston's orders to destroy the fort. When Bowie arrived at the Alamo, Colonel James C. Neill was the commander. On February 3, Bowie's old friend William Barret Travis, recently promoted to lieutenant colonel, arrived with thirty soldiers. Eight days later, Neill gave Travis command of the fort and left.

This is believed to be the only portrait of James Bowie done from life. The painter was most likely either George Peter Alexander Healy or William Edward West.

WILLIAM BARRET TRAVIS

Travis, born in South Carolina in 1809, grew up in Alabama. He became an attorney, married in 1828, and settled down in Claiborne, Alabama, where he practiced law. Two years later, suspecting his wife of being unfaithful, Travis abandoned her and went to Texas, where he settled at Anahuac, on Galveston Bay, and began to learn Spanish. There were few attorneys in the area, and Travis hoped his law practice would bring him wealth. In 1832, after being briefly imprisoned in a dispute with local authorities, Travis moved to San Felipe, where he was elected to the town council in 1834. He was appointed to lead a group of men to retake Anahuac after Mexican troops seized the town in 1835. Travis's success in this undertaking contributed to Santa Anna's decision to send General Martín Perfecto de Cos and his soldiers to occupy the Alamo. Cos called for the citizens of Texas to hand Travis over for military trial, but his demand was not met.

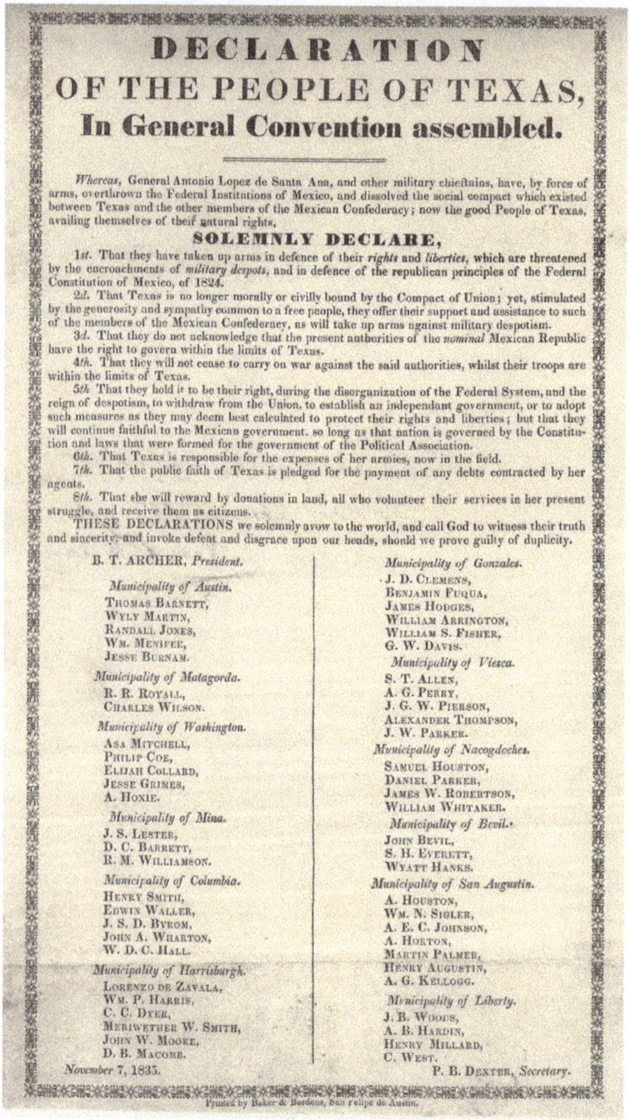

DECLARATION

OF THE PEOPLE OF TEXAS,

In General Convention assembled.

Whereas, General Antonio Lopez de Santa Ana, and other military chieftains, have, by force of arms, overthrown the Federal Institutions of Mexico, and dissolved the social compact which existed between Texas and the other members of the Mexican Confederacy; now the good People of Texas, availing themselves of their natural rights,

SOLEMNLY DECLARE,

1st. That they have taken up arms in defence of their *rights* and *liberties,* which are threatened by the encroachments of *military despots,* and in defence of the republican principles of the Federal Constitution of Mexico, of 1824.

2d. That Texas is no longer morally or civilly bound by the Compact of Union; yet, stimulated by the generosity and sympathy common to a free people, they offer their support and assistance to such of the members of the Mexican Confederacy, as will take up arms against military despotism.

3d. That they do not acknowledge that the present authorities of the *nominal* Mexican Republic have the right to govern within the limits of Texas.

4th. That they will not cease to carry on war against the said authorities, whilst their troops are within the limits of Texas.

5th That they hold it to be their right, during the disorganization of the Federal System, and the reign of despotism, to withdraw from the Union, to establish an independant government, or to adopt such measures as they may deem best calculated to protect their rights and liberties; but that they will continue faithful to the Mexican government, so long as that nation is governed by the Constitution and laws that were formed for the government of the Political Association.

6th. That Texas is responsible for the expenses of her armies, now in the field.

7th. That the public faith of Texas is pledged for the payment of any debts contracted by her agents.

8th. That she will reward by donations in land, all who volunteer their services in her present struggle, and receive them as citizens.

THESE DECLARATIONS we solemnly avow to the world, and call God to witness their truth and sincerity, and invoke defeat and disgrace upon our heads, should we prove guilty of duplicity.

B. T. ARCHER, *President.*

Municipality of Austin.
Thomas Barnett,
Wyly Martin,
Randall Jones,
Wm. Menifee,
Jesse Burnam.

Municipality of Matagorda.
R. R. Royall,
Charles Wilson.

Municipality of Washington.
Asa Mitchell,
Philip Coe,
Elijah Collard,
Jesse Grimes,
A. Hoxie.

Municipality of Mina.
J. S. Lester,
D. C. Barrett,
R. M. Williamson.

Municipality of Columbia.
Henry Smith,
Edwin Waller,
J. S. D. Byrom,
John A. Wharton,
W. D. C. Hall.

Municipality of Harrisburgh.
Lorenzo de Zavala,
Wm. P. Harris,
C. C. Dyer,
Meriwether W. Smith,
John W. Moore,
D. B. Macomb.

Municipality of Gonzales.
J. D. Clemens,
Benjamin Fuqua,
James Hodges,
William Arrington,
William S. Fisher,
G. W. Davis.

Municipality of Viesca.
S. T. Allen,
A. G. Perry,
J. G. W. Pierson,
Alexander Thompson,
J. W. Parker.

Municipality of Nacogdoches.
Samuel Houston,
Daniel Parker,
James W. Robertson,
William Whitaker.

Municipality of Bevil.
John Bevil,
S. H. Everett,
Wyatt Hanks.

Municipality of San Augustin.
A. Houston,
Wm. N. Sigler,
A. E. C. Johnson,
A. Horton,
Martin Palmer,
Henry Augustin,
A. G. Kellogg.

Municipality of Liberty.
J. B. Woods,
A. B. Hardin,
Henry Millard,
C. West.

November 7, 1835.

P. B. Dexter, *Secretary.*

Printed by Baker & Bordens, San Felipe de Austin.

In November 1835, the Consultation issued a declaration explaining why the Texians were taking arms against Mexico. Baker and Bordens printed this broadside of it. (For a transcription, please see pp. 52–53.)

Travis advised the Consultation at San Felipe in November 1835 on the formation of a cavalry for the Texas army. He accepted a commission as a lieutenant colonel, and, in January 1836, Governor Henry Smith ordered Travis to take reinforcements to the Alamo. After Colonel Neill left the fort, command of the regular army troops fell to Travis, while Bowie took command of the volunteers.

Expecting the arrival of Santa Anna's troops, Travis requested additional reinforcements. Only about thirty-five men arrived, increasing the number of defenders to between 150 and 185. On February 23, 1836, Santa Anna arrived with around 1,800 soldiers and began the siege of

BROADSIDES

Broadsides are single sheets of paper, printed only on one side, that were meant to spread information. They were posted around town or handed out to people in town squares, taverns, and churches. They were printed as quickly and cheaply as possible and were meant to be thrown away after they had served their purpose. As a result, copies of broadsides are rare today.

However, there are a number of libraries with significant collections of broadsides. These include the Library of Congress, in Washington, D.C.; Duke University, in Durham, North Carolina; and Brown University, in Providence, Rhode Island. The University of Texas at Austin's Briscoe Center for American History has an excellent collection of broadsides from Texas.

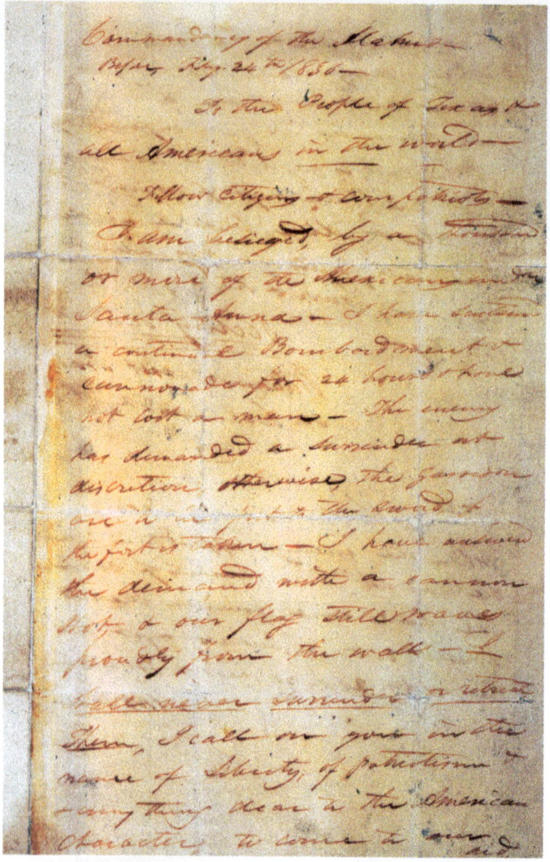

Commandancy of the Alamo—
Bejar, Feby. 24th 1836—
To the People of Texas &
all Americans in the world—
Fellow citizens & compatriots—
I am besieged, by a thousand
or more of the Mexicans under
Santa Anna— I have sustained
a continual Bombardment &
cannonade for 24 hours & have
not lost a man— The enemy
has demanded a surrender at
discretion, otherwise, the garrison
are to be put to the sword, if
the fort is taken— I have answered
the demand with a cannon
shot, & our flag still waves
proudly from the walls— I
shall never surrender or retreat.
Then, I call on you in the
name of Liberty, of patriotism &
everything dear to the American
character, to come to our aid

Travis's February 24, 1836, plea for help would inspire later generations. It is often known as the "Victory or Death Letter." (For a transcription, please see p. 53.)

the Alamo. The following day, Travis sent a letter "To the People of Texas and all Americans in the world," pleading for volunteers. In one of the most frequently quoted passages from the letter, Travis declared: "I shall never surrender or retreat. Then, I call on you in the name of Liberty, of patriotism, and everything dear to the American character, to come to our aid with all dispatch . . . If this call is neglected, I am determined to sustain myself as long as possible and die like a soldier who never forgets what is due to his own honor and that of his country—Victory or Death."

A copy of Travis's letter reached San Felipe, where the firm of Baker and Bordens printed it for distribution as a broadside. The letter was also printed in two newspapers: the *Texas Republican* printed it on March 2, 1836, and the *Telegraph & Texas Register* printed it on March 5. Hundreds of volunteers responded to Travis's plea, but none reached the Alamo in time to aid the defenders.

★ CHAPTER FOUR

THE BATTLE OF THE ALAMO

Not all of the defenders were now-famous figures like Crockett and Bowie. The majority of the defenders were Anglo, but there were also a few defenders of Mexican descent as well, including Damacio Jiménez and José María Esparza (better known as Gregorio Esparza). The youngest was sixteen-year-old William Philip King, while the oldest was fifty-six-year-old Gordon C. Jennings. Most of the defenders were in their twenties, though.

THE TEXAS DECLARATION OF INDEPENDENCE

As the defenders were readying for Santa Anna's arrival at the Alamo, the Texian community was setting up a new government for Texas. On February 1, 1836, each of the fifty-four Anglo settlements in Texas elected a delegate to attend the Convention of 1836. On March 1, while the Alamo was under siege, the delegates gathered in Washington-on-the-Brazos.

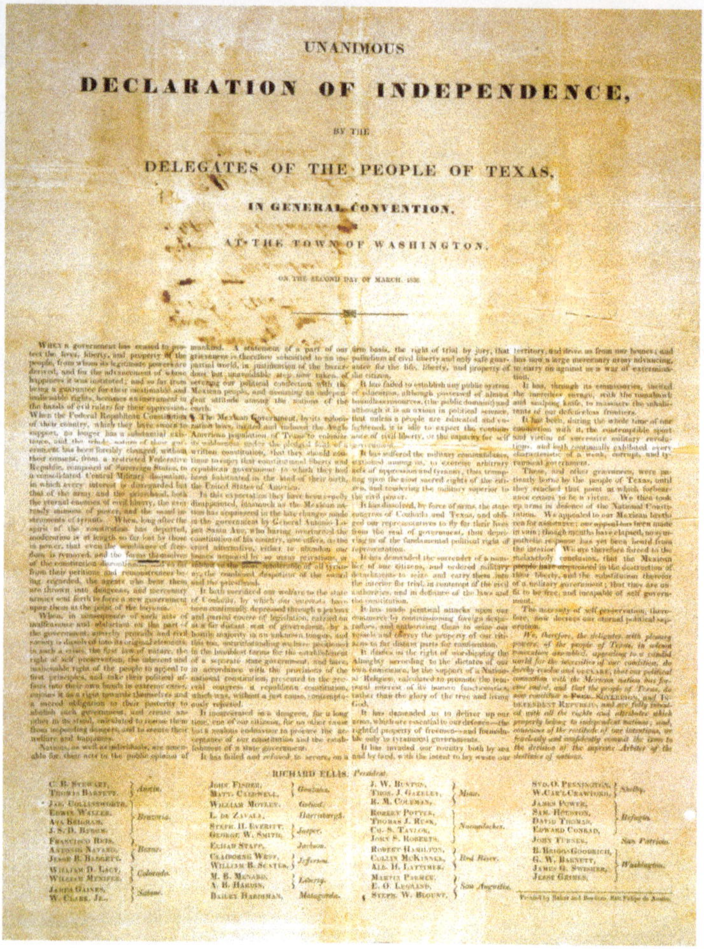
UNANIMOUS

DECLARATION OF INDEPENDENCE,

BY THE

DELEGATES OF THE PEOPLE OF TEXAS,

IN GENERAL CONVENTION,

AT THE TOWN OF WASHINGTON,

ON THE SECOND DAY OF MARCH, 1836.

RICHARD ELLIS, *President.*

This broadside of the Texas Declaration of Independence was printed by Baker and Bordens. (For a transcription, please see p. 53.)

Convention president Richard Ellis quickly appointed George C. Childress, James Gaines, Edward Conrad, Collin McKinney, and Bailey Hardeman to write the Texas Declaration of Independence. The next day, they submitted the declaration to the convention.

The Texas Declaration of Independence parallels the U.S. Declaration of Independence in many ways. It begins with statements on the duties and responsibilities of government, which the Mexican government had failed to carry out, then lists specific complaints. It concludes by stating that the people of Texas had no choice but to declare Texas a free and independent republic. The declaration was unanimously approved and signed by the delegates on March 2, 1836. They then wrote a constitution for the new republic and set up a temporary government to serve until elections could be held in October.

Copies of the Texas Declaration of Independence were sent to Béxar, Goliad, Nacogdoches, Brazoria, and San Felipe. By order of the convention, 1,000 copies were printed as broadsides by the firm of Baker and Bordens in San Felipe de Austin. In the rush to get the document printed, the names of two delegates, including George C. Childress, the declaration's author, were omitted from the list of names at the bottom. The audience for the broadsides was Americans

FALSE ADVERTISING

As the drama at the Alamo unfolded, attempts were made to rally volunteers beyond the borders of Texas. However, not all of these attempts were strictly truthful. For example, a broadside printed in New Orleans sometime after March 2, 1836, boldly proclaims that the handful of troops at the Alamo have driven back the Mexican army, killing or wounding five hundred without suffering a single loss themselves. It declares, "The wives and daughters of Texas will be saved from the brutality of Mexican soldiers." In case suspicion of the Mexicans is not enough to persuade volunteers to join the fight, each settler is promised an enormous plot of land.

The announcement goes on to state that reinforcements are headed to the Alamo and that there are enough supplies of weapons, ammunition, and provisions to guarantee the defeat of the Mexican army. The broadside was purely propaganda–none of its claims were true.

as well as Texians. The delegates knew the Texas republic would not survive without the official recognition and support of the United States.

SANTA ANNA ATTACKS

On March 5, the twelfth day of the Alamo siege and three days after the Texas Declaration of Independence was approved, Santa Anna decided it was time to attack. On Santa Anna's orders, his soldiers attacked the Alamo around 5:00 AM on March 6, 1836. The roughly 200 defenders inside the fort were no match for the almost 1,800 Mexican soldiers. Fierce cannon and rifle fire from the defenders slowed the assault only briefly.

As the Mexican forces swarmed into the Alamo, Travis was one of the first defenders to die. The Texians abandoned the walls and barricaded themselves inside the buildings. The Mexicans pursued them, and bloody hand-to-hand fighting followed. Bowie, who had fallen ill on February 24, was killed on his cot. Crockett was killed as well, though there are different stories about how he died. The battle lasted less than an hour and a half. Almost all the volunteers and regular army troops defending the Alamo died during the battle. The handful who survived were executed immediately.

Though all the defenders died, there were survivors who were allowed to go free. Santa Anna gave safe passage, a blanket, and two dollars to each woman, child, and slave inside the Alamo. Among others, these included Juana Navarro Alsbury and her sister Gertrudis Navarro, Susanna Dickinson and her daughter Angelina, and Ana Salazar Esparza and her children María de Jesús, Enrique, Manuel, and Francisco. William Travis's slave, Joe, was also among those who were spared by Santa Anna's troops.

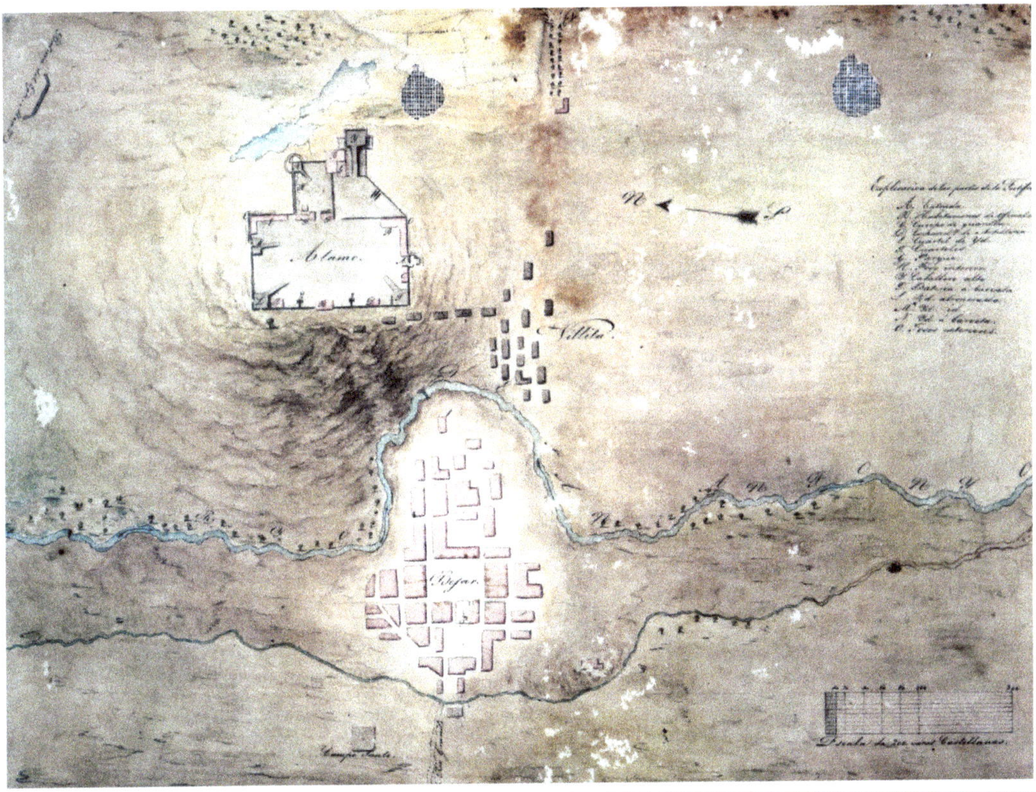

Santa Anna's battle map, seen here, was made by Ygnacio de Labastida. The 1836 map shows both the Alamo complex and San Antonio de Béxar.

The first published account of the Battle of the Alamo appeared on March 24, 1836, in the *Telegraph & Texas Register*, published in San Felipe by Baker and Bordens, the same printers who had published the Texas Declaration of Independence. The account, pieced together from different sources, included a list of those known to have been killed at the Alamo, with a promise from the publishers to print additional names as they became known.

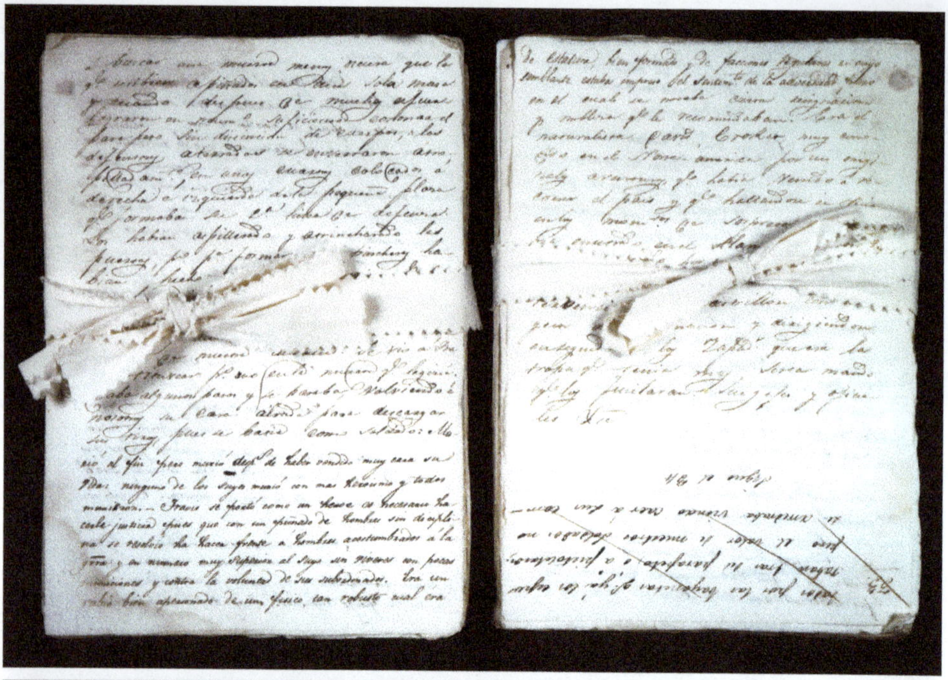

Peña's account of the battle stirred up a lot of controversy when it was first published in English in 1975. (For a transcription, please see pp. 53–54.)

Accounts of the battle by Mexican soldiers also exist. One of the best known is the memoir of Lieutenant Colonel José Enrique de la Peña. Peña expressed his admiration for the courage of the Alamo defenders, with special praise for Travis. Travis, Peña wrote, "fought like a true soldier. Finally he died, but he died after having traded his life very dearly. None of his men died with greater heroism, and they all died. Travis behaved as a hero; one must do him justice." Peña's account of Crockett's death has created great controversy among modern historians. Most people believe that Crockett died during the battle, but Peña claimed that Crockett was one of seven defenders who survived and was executed by Santa Anna.

CHAPTER FIVE

AFTER THE BATTLE

Things continued to go badly for the Texians after the Battle of the Alamo. When Sam Houston reached Gonzales on March 11, he learned about the Alamo's fall. Then Houston, many of the inhabitants of Gonzales, and the army retreated, moving northeast across the Colorado River. Houston needed time to gather his troops before they could face the Mexican army.

THE TEXAS REVOLUTION

While Houston was getting his men ready to fight, he sent orders to James Fannin at Goliad, about 80 miles (130 kilometers) southeast of the Alamo, to retreat with his five hundred soldiers. Unfortunately, several days passed before Fannin carried out Houston's order. By that time, it was too late. Santa Anna and his army caught up with Fannin's troops quickly. Rather than fight, Fannin surrendered. Santa Anna declared the Texas soldiers "pirates" and ordered them all executed.

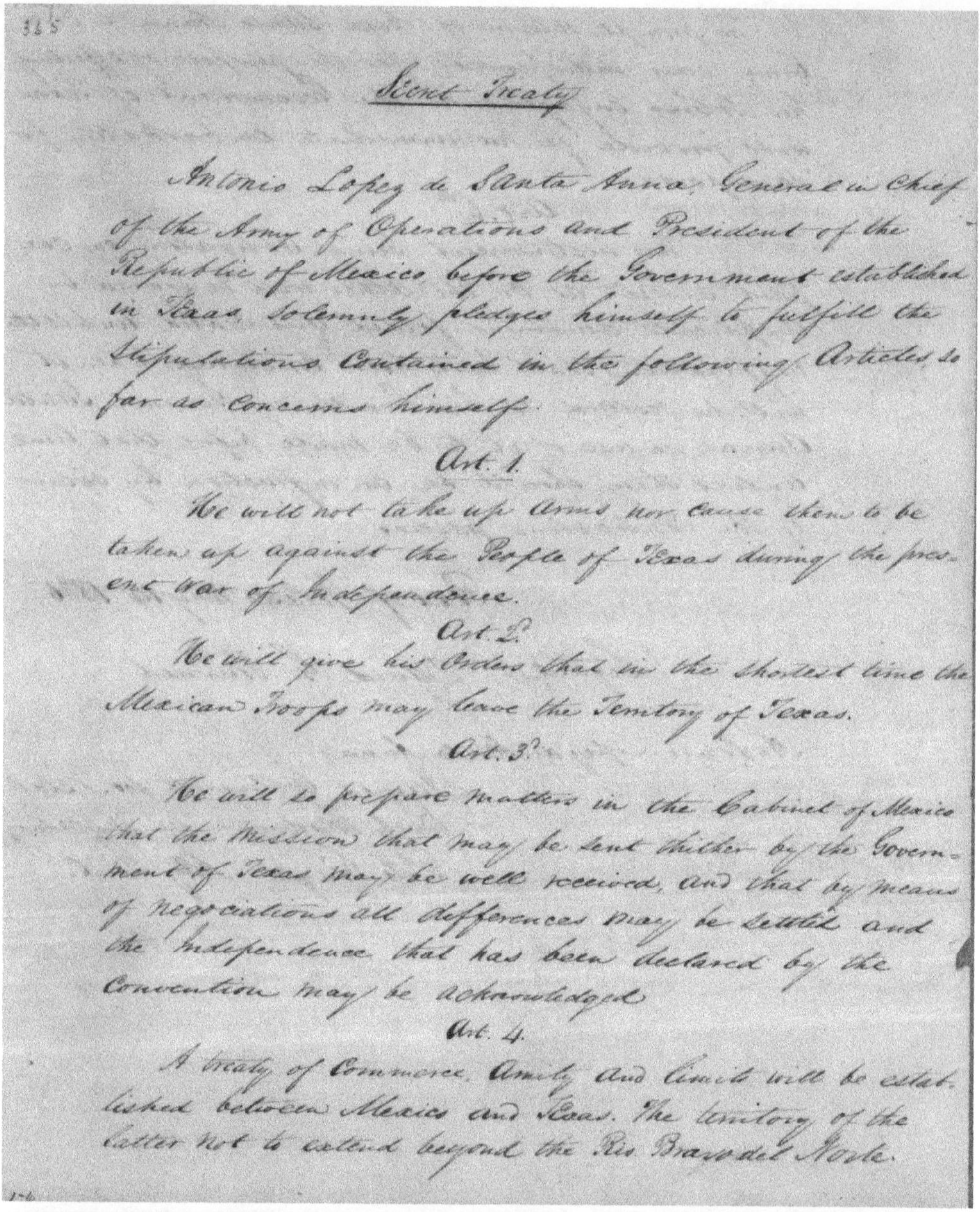

365

Secret Treaty

Antonio Lopez de Santa Anna, General in Chief of the Army of Operations and President of the Republic of Mexico before the Government established in Texas solemnly pledges himself to fulfill the stipulations contained in the following Articles so far as concerns himself.

Art. 1.

He will not take up Arms nor cause them to be taken up against the People of Texas during the present War of Independence.

Art. 2.

He will give his Orders that in the shortest time the Mexican Troops may leave the Territory of Texas.

Art. 3.

He will so prepare matters in the Cabinet of Mexico that the Mission that may be sent thither by the Government of Texas may be well received, and that by means of negociations all differences may be settled and the Independence that has been declared by the Convention may be acknowledged.

Art. 4.

A treaty of Commerce, Amity and Limits will be established between Mexico and Texas. The territory of the latter not to extend beyond the Rio Bravo del Norte.

On May 14, 1836, Santa Anna signed two treaties, one public and one secret, with the Texian government. This is the secret treaty. (For a transcription, please see page 54.)

When word of the massacre reached Houston's men, some of them fled with their families in an episode called the Runaway Scrape. On the orders of David G. Burnet, temporary president of the Republic of Texas, Houston took his remaining soldiers and headed after Santa Anna's troops. Houston's men caught up with the Mexican army on the San Jacinto River near Galveston Bay on April 20, 1836. On the afternoon of April 21, while the Mexican army enjoyed an afternoon siesta, Houston placed his men in position to attack. With cries of "Remember the Alamo!" and "Remember Goliad!" the Texas army charged the sleeping Mexicans. The bloody battle was even shorter than the fight at the Alamo had been. It lasted only eighteen minutes. When it was over, 630 Mexican soldiers had been killed and 730 had been taken prisoner. Only nine Texians were killed and thirty wounded.

With the victory in the Battle of San Jacinto, the Texians had won their independence. In September 1836, the first elections were held, and Sam Houston became the first elected president of the Republic of Texas.

Having won its independence from Mexico, Texas was now free to pursue its ultimate goal—to become a part of the United States. However, many people in the U.S. Congress opposed accepting Texas as a state. At the time, there was an uneasy balance between U.S. states in which slavery was legal and those in which it was not. Congressmen from states in which slavery was outlawed objected to the fact that slavery was legal in Texas. Adding Texas as a new U.S. state would give more power to the slaveholding states and would make it even harder to get rid of slavery in the county as a whole. It

This 1837 map of Texas was compiled by Stephen Austin and published in Philadelphia by H. S. Tanner. It shows major land grants that had been made to powerful settlers.

took almost ten years, but finally Texas became part of the United States. On December 29, 1845, President James Polk signed the paper that made Texas the twenty-eighth state. Texas formally joined the United States on February 19, 1846.

THE SURVIVORS AND FAMILIES

In the years following the Battle of the Alamo, Texas achieved what it had sought. But what happened to the survivors and the families of the defenders? One of the most famous survivors was Angelina Dickinson,

ANGELINA DICKINSON

Angelina Dickinson was born in 1834. Her life was sad and rather short. Her father, Almaron Dickinson, died at the Alamo when Angelina was not much more than a year old. Her mother, Susanna, who was only twenty-two at the time of the Battle of the Alamo, was married four more times after being widowed at the Alamo. Some of these men abused Susanna. Two of the marriages ended in divorce, and Susanna was also widowed again. This troubled family life must have been very difficult for the young Angelina. At the age of seventeen, Angelina married John Maynard Griffith. The couple had three children, but the marriage ended in divorce after six years. Angelina left her children with relatives and went to New Orleans, then to Galveston. She may have been married one or two more times there. When she was about thirty-five, she bled to death as the result of illness or injury.

known as the Babe of the Alamo because she was only fifteen months old at the time of the battle. Two stories about Angelina Dickinson and the Battle of the Alamo have been passed down over time. The first, which is probably true, is that William Barret Travis gave her a ring that had been given to him by his sweetheart. Angelina later gave the ring to a man she loved. The second story, which may or may not be true, is that Santa Anna was so charmed by the infant Angelina that he wanted to adopt her. The only source for the second story is Angelina's mother, Susanna, who told many stories about the Battle of the Alamo that are now known to be untrue.

The Republic of Texas awarded 640 acres (259 hectares) of land to all the men who had fought for Texas's independence. The families of men who died in the war, including those who were killed at the Alamo, were entitled to claim that land.

However, claiming those 640 acres (259 ha) wasn't always easy. David Crockett's widow, Elizabeth, had been left behind in Tennessee with their four children when Crockett set off to explore Texas. She did not go to Texas to claim her 640 (259 ha) acres until 1853. By the time Elizabeth Crockett arrived to claim the grant owed to her late husband, the Republic of Texas no longer existed. It was now the state of Texas. However, the state still honored claims people made for goods and services (such as military service) that they had provided to Texas when it was a republic, as long as they could prove that those claims were true. To pay the claims, the state of Texas issued Public Debt Certificates, which stated at the top that the certificates were intended to pay a public debt left over from the time when Texas was a republic.

Susanna Dickinson, seen here, became known as the Messenger of the Alamo because she carried the news of the Alamo's fall to Sam Houston.

Accompanied by three of her grown children and their families, Elizabeth spent almost a year looking for someone to accept her claim and make the necessary survey of the land she had chosen, near Acton, east of the Brazos River. Then she had to give 320 acres to the surveyor as payment. On the remaining 320 acres, her son Robert built log cabins for the extended family, and they farmed the land. Elizabeth continued to live there until her death in 1860 at the age of seventy-two.

★ CHAPTER SIX

THE LEGEND LIVES ON

The legend of the Alamo began to take root soon after the battle ended. The reports of the battle that were published in the *Telegraph & Texas Register* on March 24, 1836, painted the defenders in glowing terms, rhapsodizing, "Who would not be rather one of the Alamo heroes, than of the living of its merciless victors? Spirits of the mighty, though fallen! Honours and rest are with ye: the spark of immortality which animated your forms, shall brighten into a flame, and Texas, the whole world, shall hail ye like demigods of old, as founders of new actions, and as patterns for imitation!"

WHAT HAPPENED TO THE ALAMO?

After the fall of the Alamo, the fort was in ruins. The Republic of Texas had no use for it. In 1841, the republic returned control of the Alamo to the Catholic Church. By this time, the Alamo had become a sort of tourist attraction.

After Texas became part of the United States in 1846, control over the Alamo changed hands many times. First, the U.S. government decided that the Alamo belonged to the United States, not the Catholic Church. The army began using it as a military supply depot in 1848. However, the government and Church would argue over the ownership of the building in court for years. In 1850, the army started paying the Church rent for the use of the church. Soon after, the army began to repair and renovate the church building. They even finally added a roof. Since this pitched roof did not really work with the flat-topped façade of the old church, architect John M. Fries and stonemason David Russi designed a new campanulate, or bell-shaped, top for the façade. This rounded, hump-shaped façade is now iconic. It became the distinguishing characteristic of the building. In fact, most people today don't even realize that it was not a feature of the building at the time of the Battle of the Alamo.

After Texas voted to join the Confederacy in the months leading up to the Civil War, Texas volunteer troops seized the Alamo from the U.S. troops that were stationed there. Confederate troops occupied the fort during the Civil War. After the North won the war, the U.S. government again took over the Alamo and continued to use it until 1876.

In 1877, a French businessman named Honore Grenet established a museum and general store in the Long Barrack, one of the buildings in the Alamo compound. When the Alamo was still a mission, the Long Barrack had been the *convento*, or building where the missionaries themselves lived and worked. Grenet made grand renovations to the Long Barrack, adding porches, balconies, and a crenelated edge to the roof. For a time, he rented the church building and used it as a warehouse for his store.

In 1882, the Catholic bishop for San Antonio, John Claude Neraz, decided to sell the Alamo to raise money for other projects and offered the state of Texas the chance to buy it. On April 23, 1883, the Texas legislature passed a bill authorizing the purchase of the Alamo and placing it under the care of the city of San Antonio. Bishop Neraz's offer to sell the Alamo to the state and the deed of sale both survive.

The Long Barrack continued to be used as a store, although it had been sold to other owners after Grenet's death in 1883. In 1903, the owners considered selling the building so that it could be torn down and a hotel could be built in its place. Adina de Zavala, a San Antonio schoolteacher with an interest in preserving local history, organized an effort to save the Long Barrack. At first, de Zavala had trouble raising the necessary funds. Then a wealthy young woman named Clara Driscoll volunteered to pay the whole $75,000 selling price. In her deed for the building, Driscoll specified that she had purchased the property "for the use and benefit of the Daughters of the Republic of Texas and is to be used by them for the purpose of making a park about the Alamo."

The Daughters of the Republic of Texas (DRT) had been formed in 1891 as an organization for women who were the direct descendants of the men and women who founded the Republic of Texas. The group is still active today. Its members work to make sure that the people who struggled to make Texas free are not forgotten. They encourage historical research involving the earliest Texas documents and promote the teaching of Texas history in the public schools.

The Alamo itself remained in the care of the city of San Antonio until January 25, 1905, when the Texas legislature

This photo of Clara Driscoll dates from between 1910 and 1915. Driscoll is also known by her married name, Clara Sevier.

passed a resolution ordering the governor to transfer control of the Alamo to the DRT. Though Driscoll and de Zavala had worked together to save the Alamo, they had different ideas about what should be done with the historic site. Driscoll wanted to demolish the second story of the Long Barack to highlight the church as the centerpiece of the site. De Zavala, on the other hand, wanted to restore the Long Barrack to how it had looked at the time of the battle, pointing out that much of the fiercest fighting during the Battle of the Alamo had taken place there. Texas governor Oscar Branch Colquitt took de Zavala's side and for a while it looked like the second story of the Long Barrack would remain. However, when the governor was out of the state in 1913, the lieutenant governor authorized the razing of the structure's second story.

The Daughters of the Republic of Texas continued to be in charge of the Alamo. In 1921, they had a barrel-vaulted roof of concrete installed in the church to replace the pitched roof that had been added by the army. In 1937, the Alamo Museum was built next to the church. It was one of several museums that were built to honor Texas's centennial, or first hundred years of independence. Today, it is the Alamo Gift Shop. Also in 1937, a fire station very near the Alamo was turned over to the DRT and renamed Alamo Hall. The Daughters of the Republic of Texas Library was built next to Alamo Hall in 1950. It has since been renamed the Alamo Research Center. In 1966, the Alamo was officially listed on the National Register of Historic Places. Two years later the DRT opened the Long Barrack Museum in the former *convento*.

PRESENTING THE ALAMO

In the first images of the Alamo from after the battle, the structures are clearly in ruins. Thomas Falconer, an English lawyer and adventurer, made a watercolor sketch of the Alamo when he visited it on April 22, 1841. The church is presented as an interesting architectural ruin. Such ruins appealed to the romantic imagination of the time and had become so popular that some wealthy people in England actually had fake ruins built on their estates. Later sketches by Jacob Edmund Blake, Edward Everett, and Seth Eastman also present the Alamo as a picturesque ruin. The earliest known photograph of the church was taken in 1849. It is the only one taken before the army reconstruction. This photograph is also the earliest datable photograph taken in Texas, which shows how important a symbol the Alamo had become.

The Alamo was also celebrated in song. Robert T. Conrad's "The Alamo, or the Death of Davy Crockett" is thought to date back to 1836. In 1941, "singing cowboy" Roy Rogers released "Down by

The 1960 movie *The Alamo* cast John Wayne as Crockett, Richard Widmark as Bowie, and Laurence Harvey as Travis.

THE MCARDLE PAINTINGS

In 1870, Texas governor Edmund Davis chose painter Henry Arthur McArdle to make a series of oil paintings showing battles and heroes of the Texas War for Independence. One of the paintings, titled *Dawn at the Alamo*, shows the Battle of the Alamo. McArdle did a lot of research for the painting. He tried to find out what the landscape around the Alamo had looked like, what uniforms the soldiers had worn, and what equipment each army had used. He looked for portraits or photographs of the famous people involved so that he could make accurate likenesses of them. McArdle even contacted General Santa Anna to ask if he could provide any additional information about the battle.

In spite of McArdle's extensive research, his painting is more an interpretation of the event than a factual portrayal of it. He made the defenders look noble and the Mexican soldiers look villainous. He used light to draw special attention to William Barret Travis, David Crockett, and James Bowie, and presented them in heroic poses. He even placed Bowie in the thick of the battle (Bowie had actually been too ill to join the fight and had been killed while lying on his cot). In contrast, the Mexican soldiers have exaggerated features and assume poses that are definitely not heroic.

McArdle's *Battle of San Jacinto* also glorifies the Texas soldiers. Both paintings are impressively large: *Dawn at the Alamo* is about 7 feet (2.1 meters) tall and 12 feet (3.7 meters) wide, while the *Battle of San Jacinto* is about 8 feet (2.4 meters) tall and 14 feet (4.3 meters) wide. Today, the paintings hang in the Senate Chamber in the Texas Capitol.

the Old Alamo." In the 1950s and 1960s, several groups recorded versions of Jane Bowers's "Remember the Alamo."

A number of movies about the Alamo were made, too. In 1914, a silent film called *The Siege and Fall of the Alamo* became a hit. It would be one of the few movies actually filmed at the Alamo. *The Alamo*, released in 1960, featured a heroic John Wayne. *Viva Max!* was a 1969 comedy that revolved around a Mexican general's plot to retake the Alamo. *The Alamo*, from 2004, tried to demystify the heroes a bit. The Alamo has also been featured on television: the TV movie *The Alamo: Thirteen Days to Glory* aired

Many events take place at the Alamo each year, including the Veterans Day ceremony seen here. The anniversary of the battle and San Antonio Founder's Day also feature special commemorations.

in 1987, while the miniseries *James A. Michener's Texas* debuted in 1995.

THE ALAMO TODAY

In the 1980s, there were disagreements between the DRT on one hand and the city and state on the other over plans to redesign Alamo Plaza. These tensions flared up again in the first decade of the twentieth century, when there were disputes over the Alamo trademark and repairs to the church building. In 2011, the Texas State Legislature officially turned authority over the Alamo to the Texas General Land Office. The DRT continued to be involved, though, since the General Land Office signed an agreement to have the DRT oversee the daily operation of the site.

The Alamo continues to draw more than 2.5 million visitors each year. Today, anyone can visit the Alamo and see the historical documents and objects there. Visitors learn the true facts about the Battle of the Alamo and can also explore how the Alamo's defenders became symbols of the eternal human struggle for liberty. On one hand, the legend has given the Alamo defenders a kind of immortality. On the other hand, it has obscured a deeper understanding and appreciation of the real flesh-and-blood men who fought and died at the fort.

TIMELINE

1519 Alonso Álvarez de Pineda is the first Spanish explorer to reach Texas.

1718 Spanish soldiers and missionaries set up the Mission San Antonio de Valero near the San Antonio River.

1793 Mission San Antonio de Valero is secularized.

1803 Spanish soldiers from the Mexican village of El Alamo move into the mission, which now becomes known as the Alamo.

1821 Mexico gains independence from Spain. It grants Moses Austin permission to bring Anglo settlers into Texas, but he dies before he can do so.

1822 Austin's son, Stephen, carries out his father's plan.

1830 Worried that U.S. settlers outnumber Mexicans in Texas, the Mexican government bans further Anglo settlement.

1833 General Antonio López de Santa Anna is elected president of the Republic of Mexico.

1834 Santa Anna decides that Mexico is not ready for democratic rule and makes himself dictator.

1835 Anglo settlers drive Mexican soldiers from the Alamo, leaving Texas under the control of the U.S. settlers.

1836 Texas declares independence from Mexico. The Mexican army defeats the settlers at the Battle of the Alamo. Texas wins its independence when it defeats Mexican forces at the Battle of San Jacinto. On April 20, it becomes the Republic of Texas.

1841 The Republic of Texas returns control of the Alamo to the Catholic Church. Tourists begin to visit the site.

1846 Texas becomes a U.S. state.

1905 The Daughters of the Republic of Texas becomes responsible for the care of the Alamo.

2011 Custodianship of the Alamo is transferred to the Texas General Land Office.

TRANSLATION OF AN EXCERPT FROM A LETTER FROM AMBROSIO MARÍA DE ALDASORO TO ANTONIO MARÍA MARTÍNEZ, JANUARY 17, 1821

Dear Sir:
In all the meetings we have had, I have born in mind the needs of the province, and as I offered to you and its population, to help, with all my effort, listening to this Superior Chief of the Provincial Government, to secure the move of the neighbors of Misuri, in accordance with your desires. I have tried, with all my effort as I said, to dispose the government to accede to the request of the interested person. In this same mail this permission is granted; and anyway congratulations on your management of this.

EXCERPT FROM PROCLAMATION OF SAM. HOUSTON, COMMANDER-IN-CHIEF OF THE ARMY OF TEXAS, DECEMBER 12, 1835

The services of five thousand volunteers will be accepted. By the first of March next, we must meet the enemy with an army worthy of our cause, and which will reflect honor upon freemen. Our habitations must be defended; the sanctity of our hearths and firesides must be preserved from pollution. Liberal Mexicans will unite with us. Our countrymen in the field have presented an example worthy of imitation. Generous and brave hearts from a land of freedom have joined our standard before Bejar. They have, by their heroism and valor called forth the admiration of their comrades in arms, and have reflected additional honor on the land of their birth.

Let the brave rally to our standard!

SAM. HOUSTON,
Commander-in-chief of the Army.
By order,
George W. Poe,
Acting Adjutant-General.

DECLARATION OF THE PEOPLE OF TEXAS, IN GENERAL CONVENTION ASSEMBLED, NOVEMBER 7, 1835

Whereas, General Antonio Lopez de Santa Anna, and other military chieftains, have, by force of arms, overthrown the federal institutions of Mexico, and dissolved the social compact which existed between Texas and the other members of the Mexican confederacy; now the good people of Texas, availing themselves of their natural rights,

SOLEMNLY DECLARE,

1st. That they have taken up arms in defence of their rights and liberties, which were threatened by the encroachments of military despots, and in defence of the republican principles of the federal constitution of Mexico, of eighteen and twenty-four.

2d. That Texas is no longer morally or civilly bound by the compact of union; yet, stimulated by the generosity and sympathy common to a free people, they offer their support and assistance to such of the members of the Mexican confederacy as will take up arms against military despotism.

3d. That they do not acknowledge that the present authorities of the nominal Mexican republic have the right to govern within the limits of Texas.

4th. That they will not cease to carry on war against the said authorities whilst their troops are within the limits of Texas.

5th. That they hold it to be their right during the disorganization of the federal system, and the reign of despotism, to withdraw from the union, to establish an independent government, or to adopt such measures as they may deem best calculated to protect their rights and liberties, but that they will continue faithful to the Mexican government so long as that nation is governed by the constitution and laws that were formed for the government of the political association.

6th. That Texas is responsible for the expense of her armies now in the field.

7th. That the public faith of Texas is pledged for the payment of any debts contracted by her agents.

8th. That she will reward, by donations in lands, all who volunteer their services in her present struggle, and receive them as citizens.

These declarations we solemnly avow to the world, and call God to witness their truth and sincerity, and invoke defeat and disgrace upon our heads, should we prove guilty of duplicity.

EXCERPT FROM WILLIAM BARRET TRAVIS'S LETTER FROM THE ALAMO, FEBRUARY 24, 1836

To the People of Texas & all Americans in the world—

Fellow citizens & compatriots—

I am besieged, by a thousand or more of the Mexicans under Santa Anna—I have sustained a continual Bombardment & cannonade for 24 hours & have not lost a man—The enemy has demanded a surrender at discretion, otherwise, the garrison are to be put to the sword, if the fort is taken—I have answered the demand with a cannon shot, & our flag still waves proudly from the walls—I shall never surrender or retreat. Then, I call on you in the name of Liberty, of patriotism & everything dear to the American character, to come to our aid.

EXCERPT FROM THE TEXAS DECLARATION OF INDEPENDENCE, MARCH 2, 1836

When long after the spirit of the constitution has departed, moderation is at length so far lost by those in power, that even the semblance of freedom is removed, and the forms themselves of the constitution discontinued, and so far from their petitions and remonstrances being regarded, the agents who bear them are thrown into dungeons, and mercenary armies sent forth to force a new government upon them at the point of the bayonet.

When, in consequence of such acts of malfeasance and abdication on the part of the government, anarchy prevails, and civil society is dissolved into its original elements, in such a crisis, the first law of nature, the right of self preservation, the inherent and inalienable right of the people to appeal to first principles, and take their political affairs into their own hands in extreme cases, enjoins it as a right towards themselves and a sacred obligation to their posterity to abolish such government, and create another in its stead, calculated to rescue them from impending dangers, and to secure their welfare and happiness.

EXCERPT FROM JOSÉ ENRIQUE DE LA PEÑA'S ACCOUNT OF THE BATTLE OF THE ALAMO, 1830S

Some seven men had survived the general carnage and, under the protection of General Castrillón, they were brought before Santa Anna. Among them was one of great stature, well proportioned, with regular features, in whose face there was the imprint of adversity, but in whom one also noticed a degree of resignation and nobility that did him honor. He was the naturalist David Crockett, well known in North America for his unusual adventures, who had undertaken to explore the country and who, finding himself in Béjar at the very moment of surprise, had taken refuge in the Alamo, fearing that his status as a foreigner might not be respected. Santa Anna answered Castrillón's intervention in Crockett's behalf with a gesture of indignation and, addressing himself to the sappers, the troops closest to him, ordered his execution. The commanders and officers were outraged at this action and did not support the order, hoping that once the fury of the moment had blown over these men would be spared; but several officers who were around the president and who, perhaps, had not been present during the moment of danger, became noteworthy by an infamous deed, surpassing the soldiers in cruelty. They thrust themselves forward, in order to flatter their commander, and with swords in hand, fell upon these unfortunate, defenseless men just as a tiger leaps upon his prey. Though tortured before they were killed, these unfortunates died without complaining and without humiliating themselves before their torturers.

EXCERPT FROM THE SECRET TREATY OF VELASCO, MAY 14, 1836 SECRET TREATY

Antonio Lopez de Santa Anna, General in Chief of the Army of Operations and President of the Republic of Mexico, before the Government established in Texas, solemnly pledges himself to fulfill the stipulations contained in the following Articles, so far as concerns himself.

Art. 1.

He will not take up arms nor cause them to be taken up against the People of Texas during the present War of Independence.

Art. 2d.

He will give his Orders that in the shortest time the Mexican Troops may leave the Territory of Texas.

Art. 3d.

He will so prepare matters in the Cabinet of Mexico that the Mission that may be sent thither by the Government of Texas, may be well received, and that by means of negociations all differences may be settled and the Independence that has been declared by the Convention may be acknowledged

Art. 4.

A treaty of Commerce, Amity and limits will be established between Mexico and Texas. The territory of the latter not to extend beyond the Rio. Bravo del Norte.

GLOSSARY

almanac An annual publication containing general information about someone or something.

Anglo A short form of the Spanish word *angloamericano*, applied to white people in North America who are not of Spanish descent.

barricade To put up barriers to block an enemy's advance.

buffer A zone separating two groups from each other.

commission An appointment to military rank and authority.

dictator Someone who rules with absolute power.

exaggerate To distort something, often in an unflattering way, by making it larger than normal.

glorify To elevate someone or something by bestowing lavish honor and praise.

irrigation The carrying of water to land through ditches or pipes.

land speculator A person who buys land hoping to sell it to someone else for a much higher price.

legislature A body of people that has the power to make or pass laws.

massacre The killing of a large number of people, especially when it seems unjustified.

militia A group of citizens who are not soldiers but who have been organized for military service.

propaganda The spreading of ideas and information, not necessarily true, to help one's own cause or to hurt an enemy's cause.

reinforcements Additional soldiers to increase the number of soldiers at a specific location.

secularize To turn the control over something from religious authorities to nonreligious ones.

siege A military blockade around a city or fort to force it to surrender.

strategic Related to the science of planning and directing large military movements.

Texian A settler of Texas when it was part of Mexico or the Republic of Texas, in particular used to refer to settlers from the United States.

volunteer A person who offers himself or herself for service in the military of his or her own free will.

FOR MORE INFORMATION

The Alamo
300 Alamo Plaza
San Antonio, TX 78205
(210) 225-1391
Website: http://www.thealamo.org
There is no better place to learn about the Alamo than at the historic site itself. Visitors to the 4.2-acre (1.7 ha) site will learn about the famous 1936 battle, as well as other interesting periods in the site's over 300-year history.

The Bullock Texas State History Museum
1800 Congress Avenue
Austin, TX 78701
(512) 936-8746
Website: http://www.thestoryoftexas.com
This museum aims to tell the story of Texas's history. It features special exhibits, rare documents, two movie theaters, and more. The museum website features the Texas Story Project, as well as information on exhibitions, a Texas history timeline, and an interactive map.

The Daughters of the Republic of Texas
510 E. Anderson Lane
Austin, TX 78752
(512) 339-1997
Website: http://www.drtinfo.org
This organization, founded in 1891, aims to "perpetuate the memory and spirit of the men and women who achieved and maintained the independence of Texas." The DRT manages the daily operations at the Alamo and has custodianship of the French Legation Museum in Austin.

San Antonio Living History Association
5310 San Pedro Avenue
San Antonio, TX 78212
(210) 201-6653
Website: http://salha.org
This group hopes to foster an appreciation for Texas's past through living history programs, demonstrations, and reenactments of key historical events. Among other activities, it has presented several living history reenactment events in Alamo Plaza.

San Antonio Missions National Historical Park
Administrative Headquarters
2202 Roosevelt Avenue
San Antonio, TX 78210
(210) 922-0543
Website: http://www.nps.gov/saan/index.htm
This national historical park is comprised of Mission Concepción, Mission San José, Mission San Juan, and Mission Espada. Visitors can learn what life on a Texas mission was like. The park's visitor center is located at Mission San José, which also features a gristmill.

Texas Heritage Society
1949 Lynnview Drive
Houston, TX 77055
(832) 326-0835
Website: http://www.texasheritagesociety.org
This group's goal is to "promote the history and genealogy of Texas, particularly of South and Southeast Texas." It sponsors a scholarly journal called the *Journal of Texas Heritage.*

Texas Historical Foundation
P.O. Box 50314
Austin, TX 78763
(512) 453-2154
Website: http://texashistoricalfoundation.org
Established in 1954, this independent organization supports research in Texas history, as well as the preservation of historical and prehistoric artifacts. The group's main contributions are raising funds, providing historical preservation grants, and publishing *Texas Heritage Magazine.*

Texas State Historical Association
1155 Union Circle #311580
Denton, TX 76203
(940) 369-5200
Website: http://www.tshaonline.org
Formed in 1897, this group's goal is to keep Texas history alive. Its press puts out volumes on Texas history and publishes the *Southwestern Historical Quarterly*, a well-respected scholarly journal. You can use the group's website to access *The Handbook of Texas*, a comprehensive resource for information about the state's history.

WEBSITES

Because of the changing nature of Internet links, Rosen Publishing has developed an online list of websites related to the subject of this book. This site is updated regularly. Please use this link to access the list:

http://www.rosenlinks.com/UAH/Alamo

FOR FURTHER READING

Belviso, Meg, and Pamela D. Pollack. *What Was the Alamo?* New York, NY: Grosset & Dunlap, 2013.

Christian, Betsy, and George Christian. *For the Love of Texas: Tell Me About the Revolution!* Charleston, SC: The History Press, 2013.

Davis, William C. *Three Roads to the Alamo: The Lives and Fortunes of David Crockett, James Bowie, and William Barret Travis.* New York, NY: Harper Perennial, 1999.

Donovan, James. *The Blood of Heroes: The 13-Day Struggle for the Alamo—and the Sacrifice That Forged a Nation.* New York, NY: Little, Brown and Company, 2012.

Harasymiw, Therese. *Causes and Effects of the Texas Revolution* (Spotlight on Texas). New York, NY: Rosen Publishing, 2010.

Hoffman, Mary Ann. *The Alamo* (Spotlight on Texas). New York, NY: Rosen Publishing, 2010.

Levy, Janey. *Native Americans in Texas* (Spotlight on Texas). New York, NY: Rosen Publishing, 2010.

McDonald, L. Lloyd. *Tejanos in the 1835 Texas Revolution.* Gretna, LA: Pelican Publishing Company, 2009.

Mountjoy, Shane. *The Alamo: The Battle for Texas* (Milestones in American History). New York, NY: Chelsea House Publishers, 2008.

Nardo, Don. *The Alamo* (World History). San Diego, CA: Lucent Books, 2012.

Walker, Paul Robert. *Remember the Alamo: Texians, Tejanos, and Mexicans Tell Their Stories.* Washington, DC: National Geographic Children's Books, 2007.

Zaboly, Gary S. *An Altar for Their Sons: The Alamo and the Texas Revolution in Contemporary Newspaper Accounts.* Buffalo Gap, TX: State House Press, 2011.

N

P

R

S

T

Z

ABOUT THE AUTHORS

Susanna Keller has written several books on American history for young readers, including *The True Story of Lewis and Clark* and *The True Story of Paul Revere's Ride*. She has been fascinated by American history since childhood.

Janey Levy has a Ph.D. in art history from the University of Kansas. She has taught art history classes at several colleges and universities, published articles and essays on art history, and curated two art exhibits. Levy and her family, including two dogs, two cats, and assorted fish, live in the countryside near Buffalo, New York. She has written several books for the Rosen Publishing Group's classroom division, including the series Primary Sources in Early American History.

PHOTO CREDITS

Cover MPI/Archive Photos/Getty Images; p. 3 Lone Wolf Photography/Shutterstock.com; pp. 4–5 (background) Enigmangels/Shutterstock.com; pp. 6, 13, 20 (background), 27, 33, 41 Rose West Photo/Shutterstock.com; p. 7 Courtesy of the Wittliff Collections, Texas State University; pp. 8, 20 (inset) Private Collection/Peter Newark American Pictures/Bridgeman Images; p. 11 Universal History Archive/Universal Images Group/Getty Images; pp. 14, 15, 28, 31, 32 Center for American History, The University of Texas at Austin; p. 18 Western Americana Collection, Beinecke Library, Yale University; pp. 19, 26, 34, 39 Texas State Library & Archives Commission; p. 23 State Preservation Board, Austin, Texas; p. 24 The Dolph Briscoe Center for American History, The University of Texas at Austin; p. 36 Historic Map Works LLC/Getty Images; p. 44 Library of Congress Prints and Photographs Division; p. 46 Courtesy Everett Collection; p. 48 © James Southers/Alamy; cover, p. 1 design elements Piotr Krzeslak/Shutterstock.com (flag), Aleksandrs Bondars/Shutterstock.com (scroll); cover and interior pages background textures chudo-yudo/Shutterstock.com, Alina G/Shutterstock.com, Attitude/Shutterstock.com, sl_photo/Shutterstock.com

Designer: Michael Moy; Editor: Amelie von Zumbusch